MORE BOOK, FREEBIE PAGES : K-IMAGINE-PUB.COM

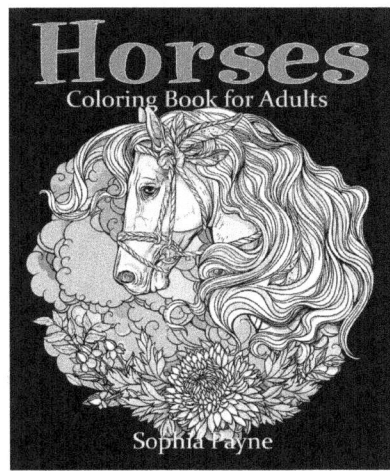
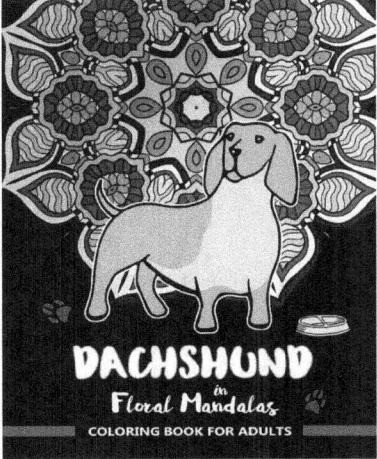
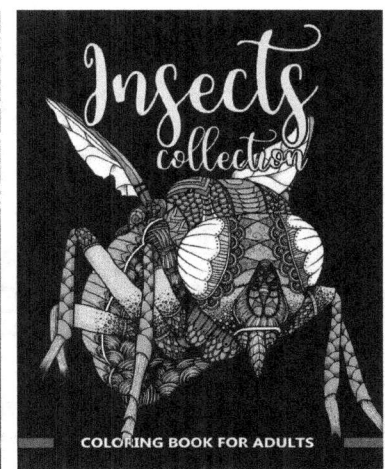
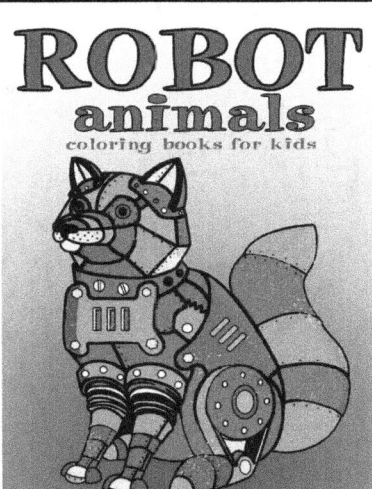
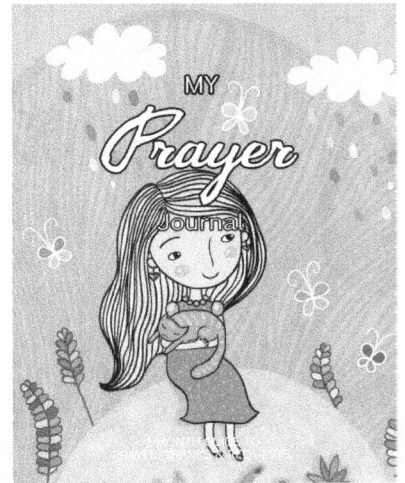
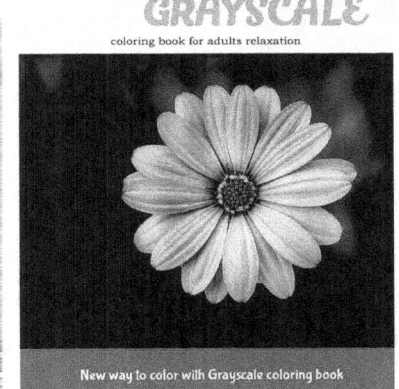
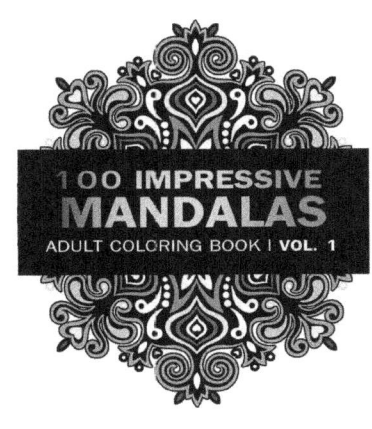
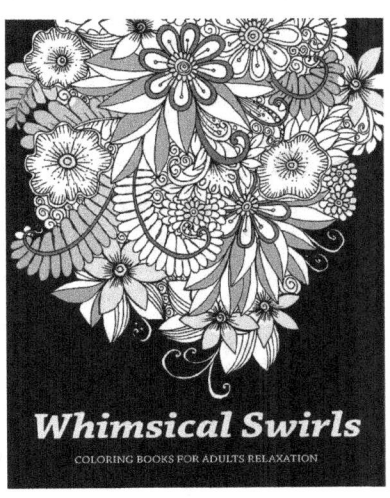
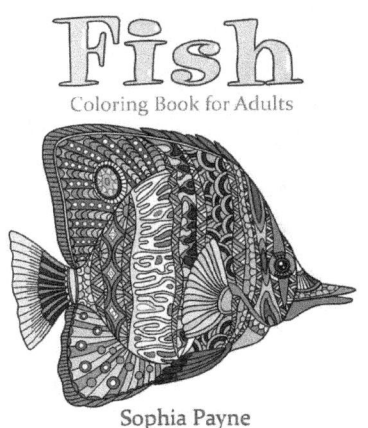

Copyright: Published in the United States

Copyright: Published in the United States

All rights reserved.

- Color Test Page -

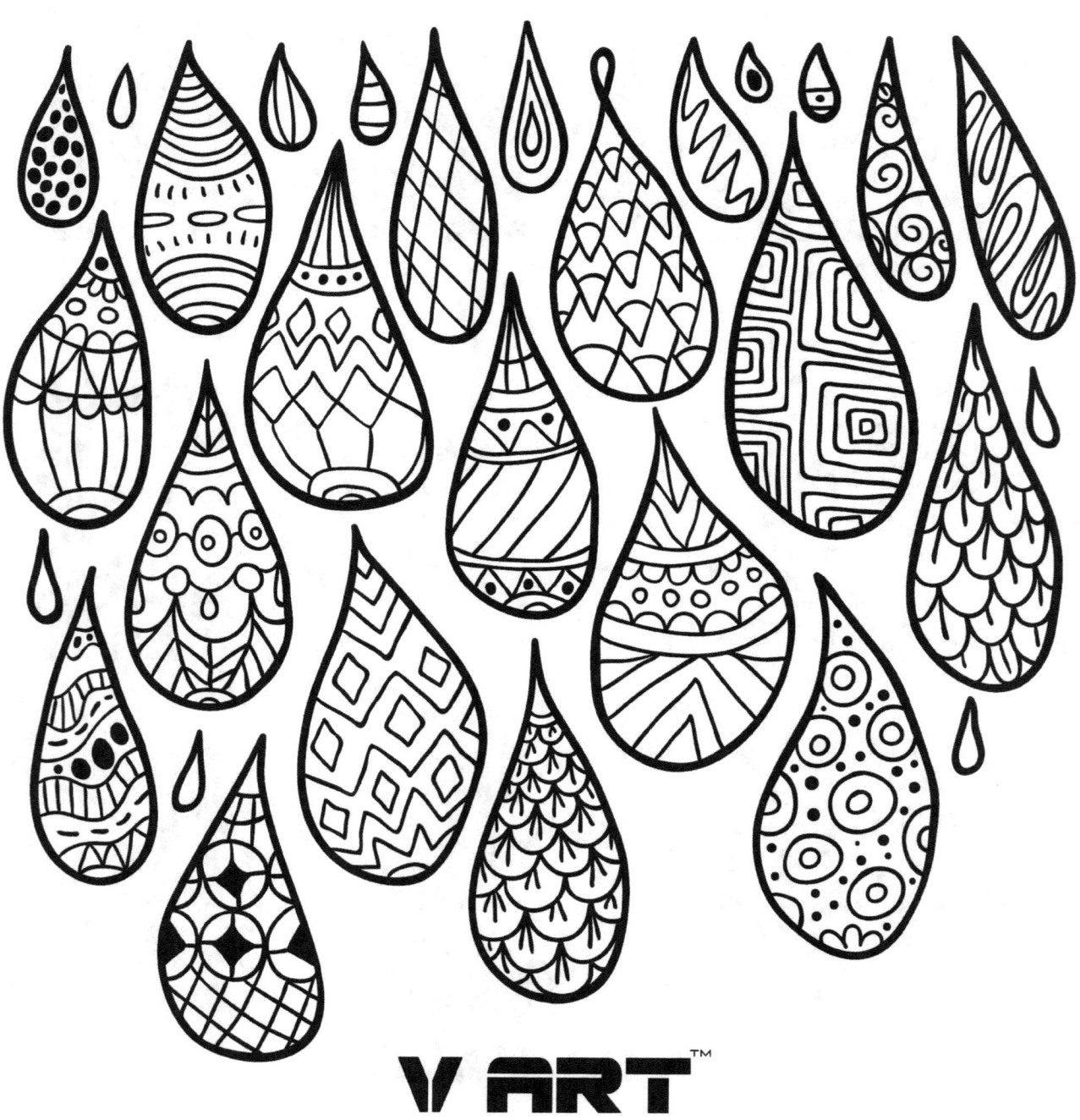

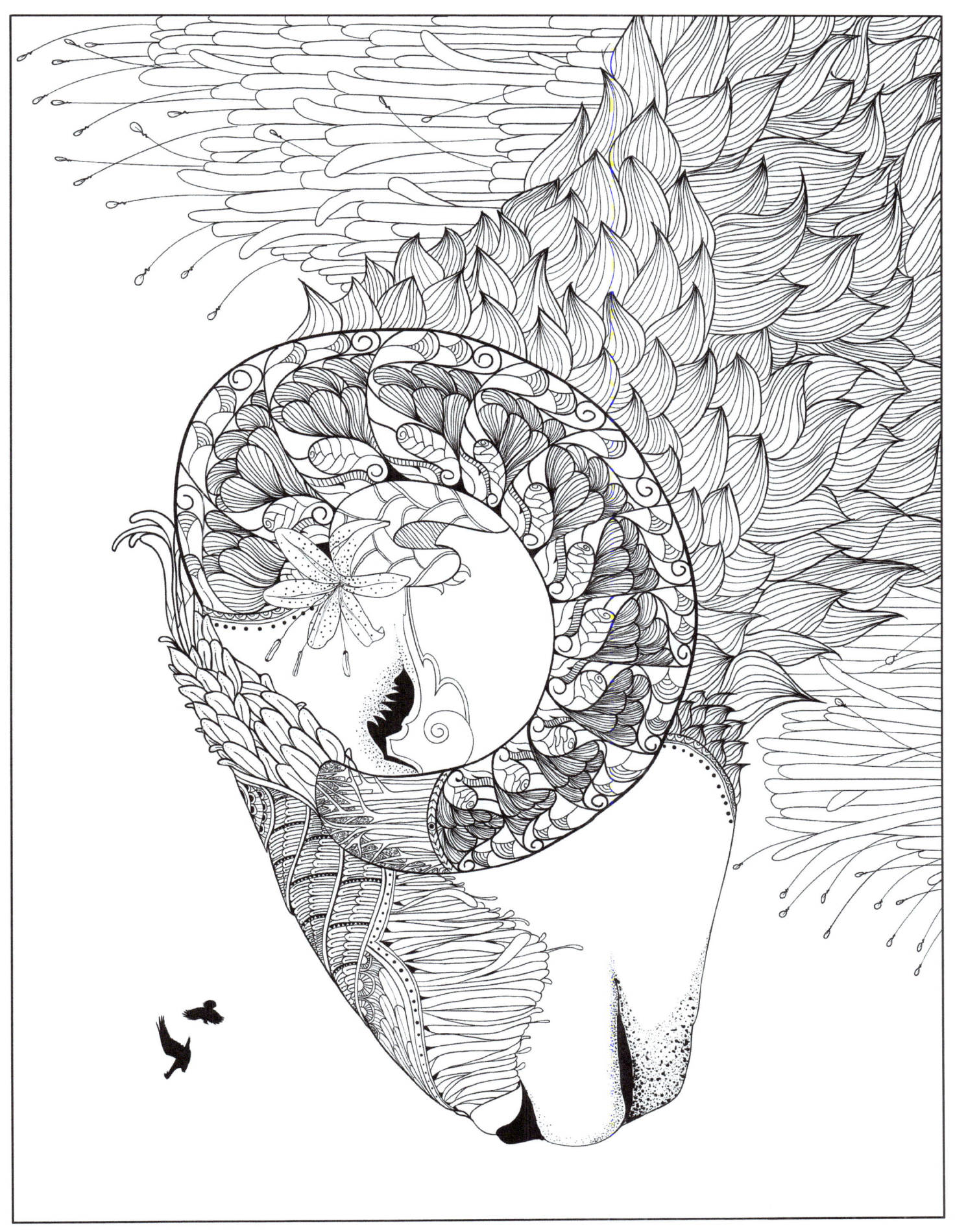

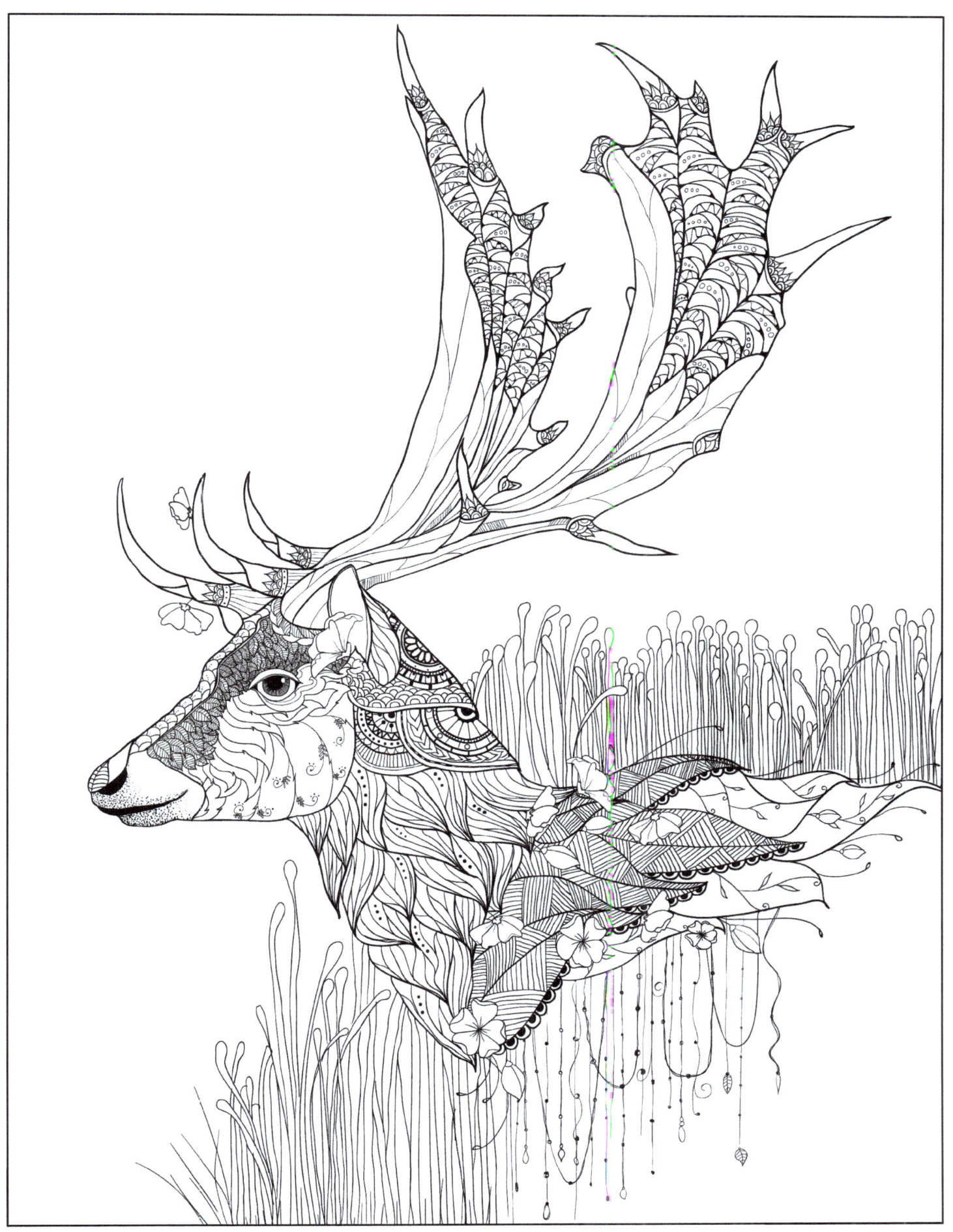

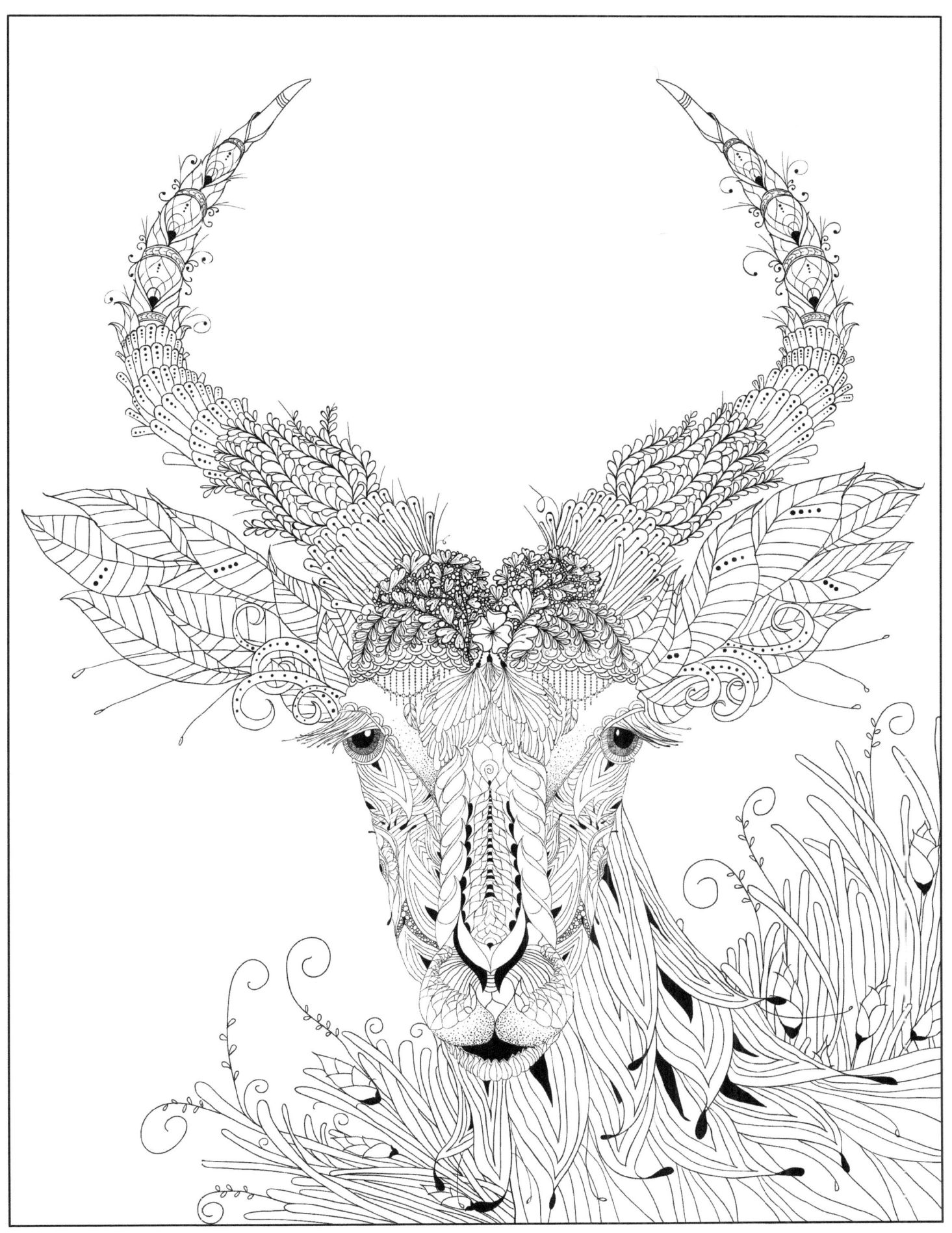

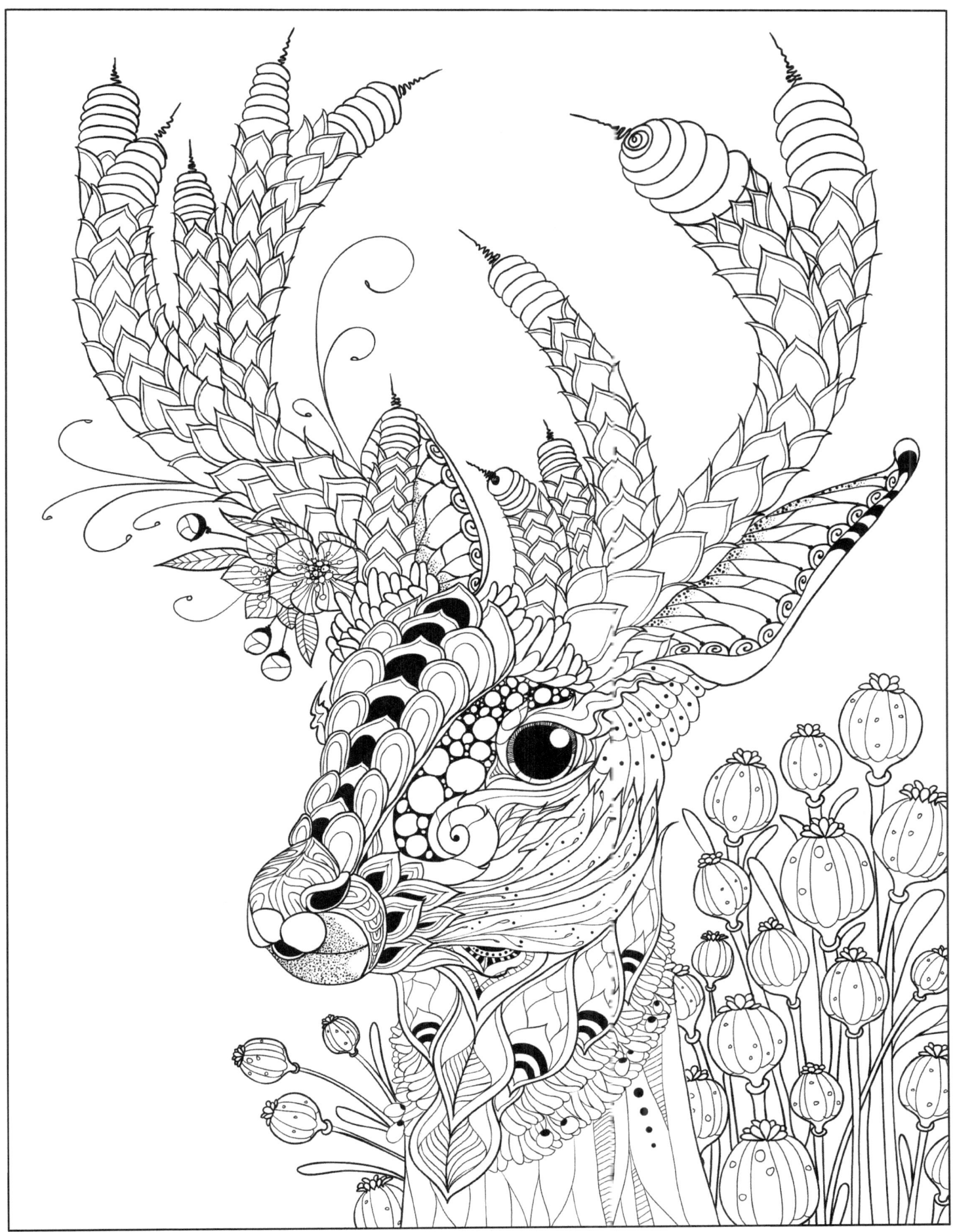

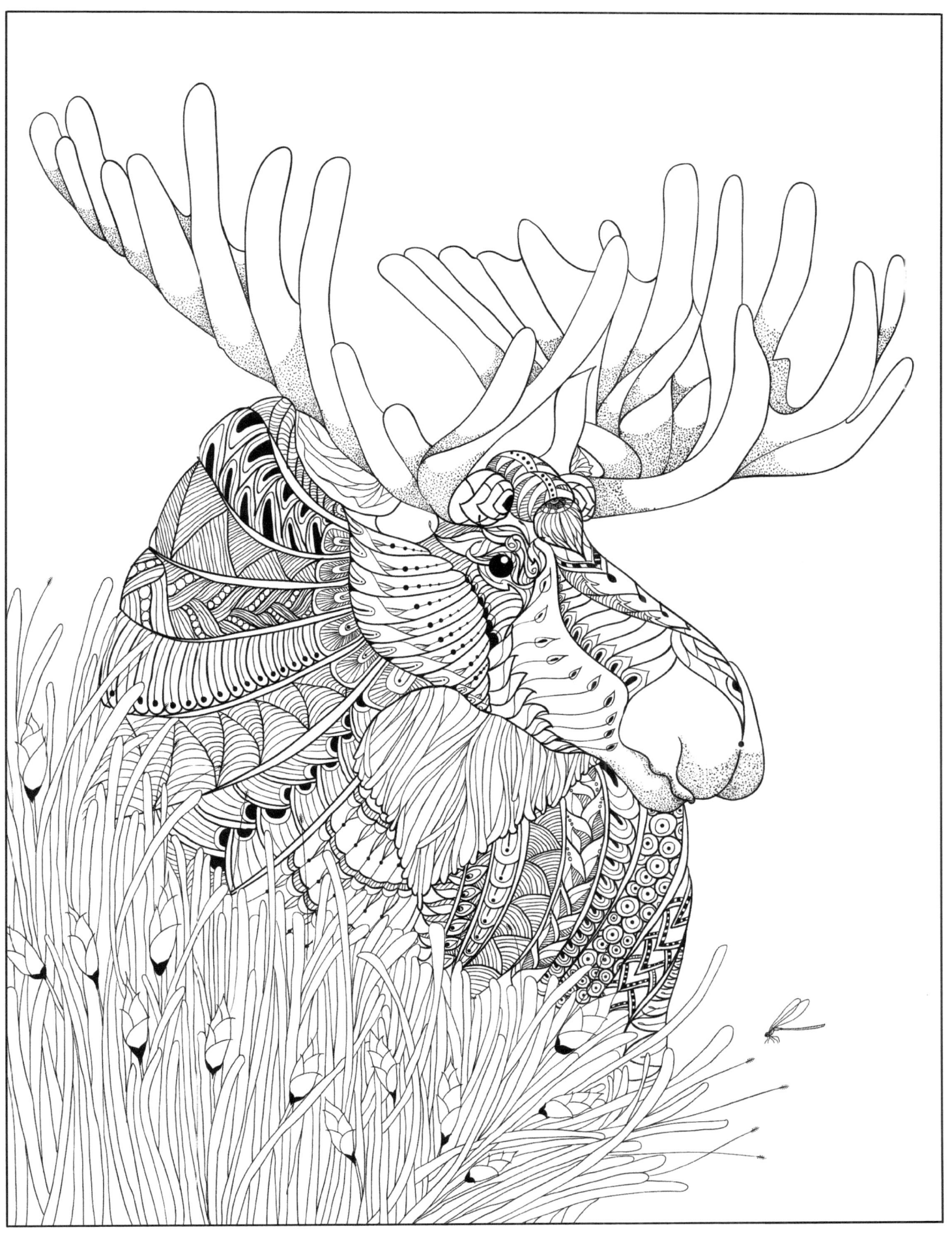

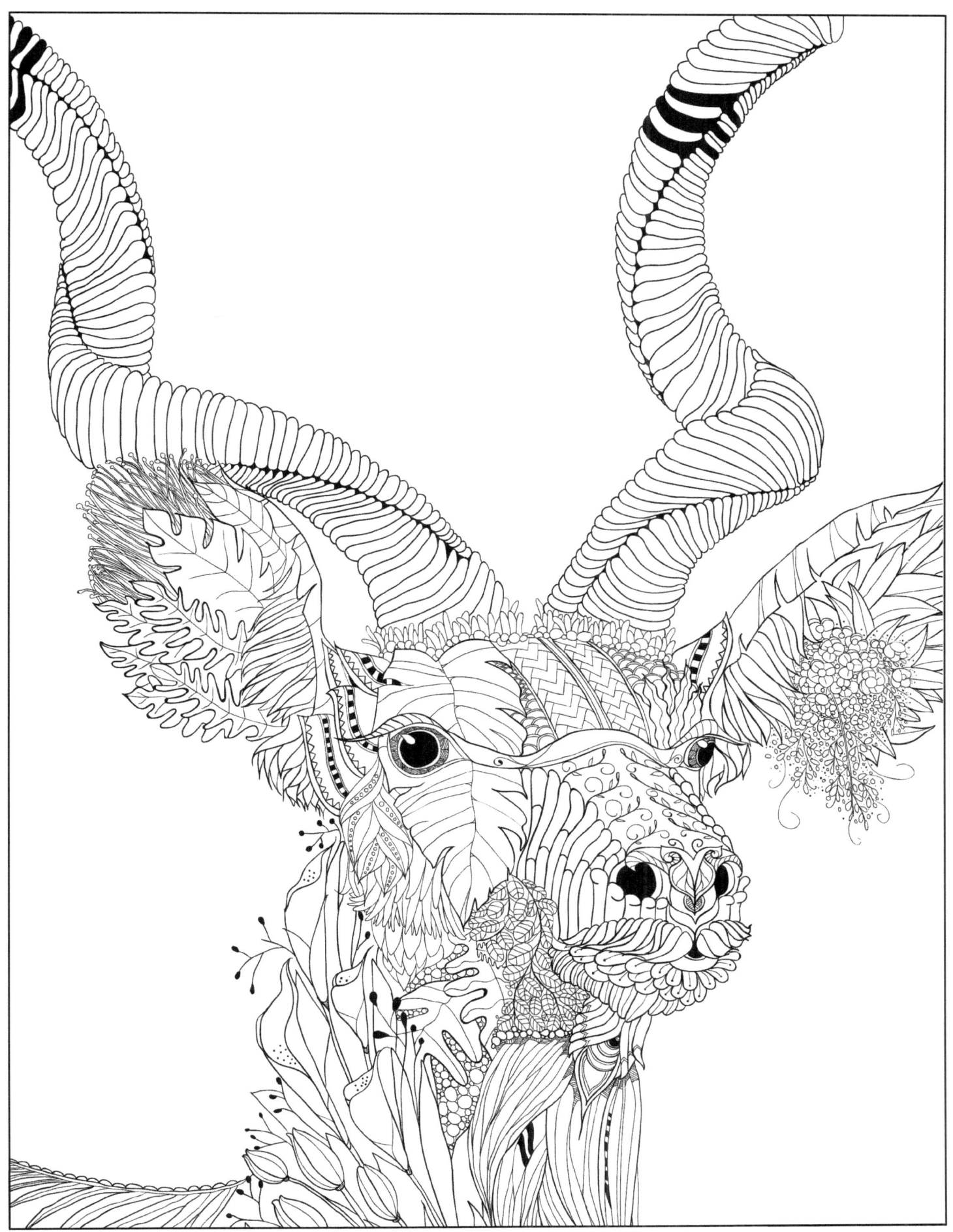

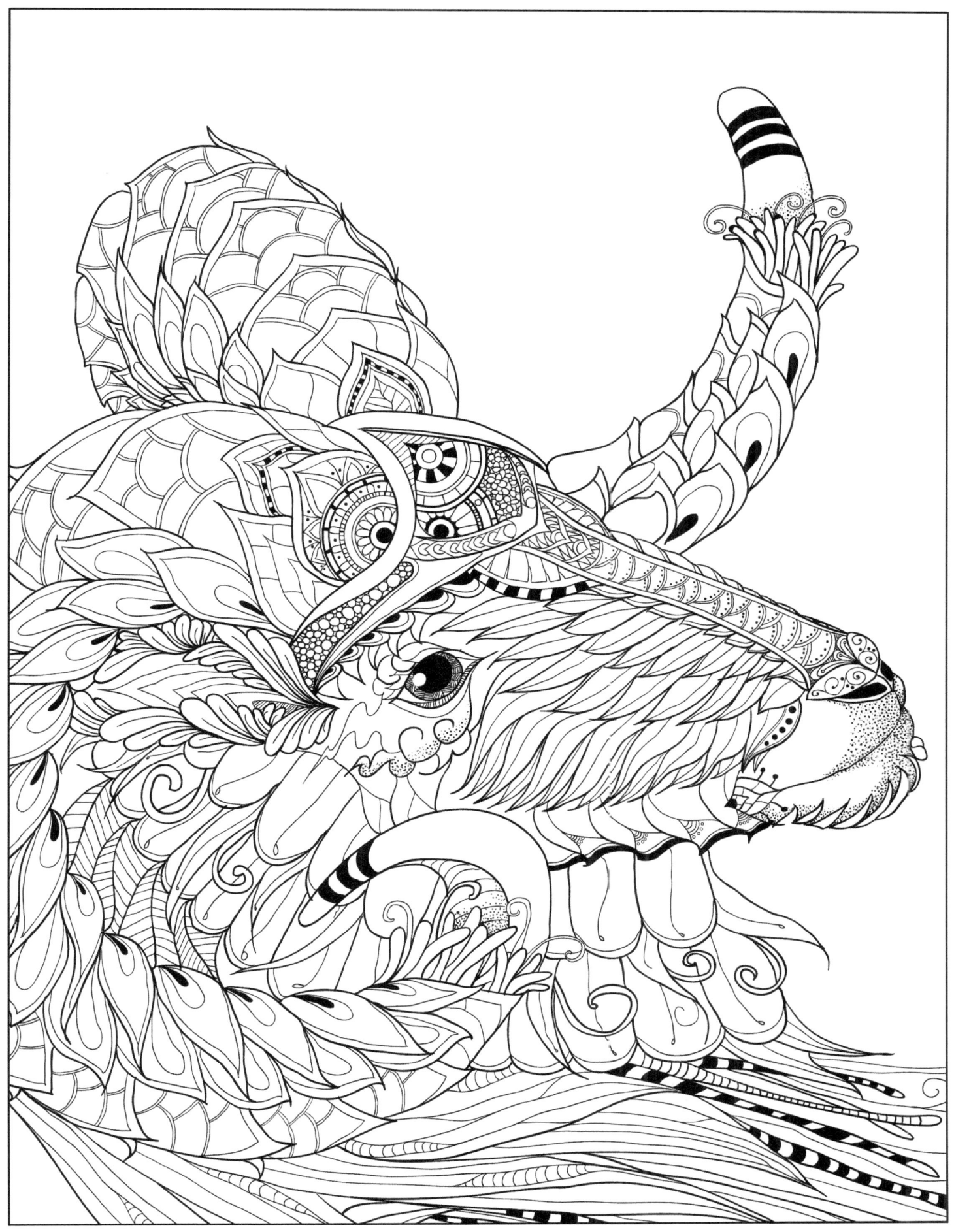

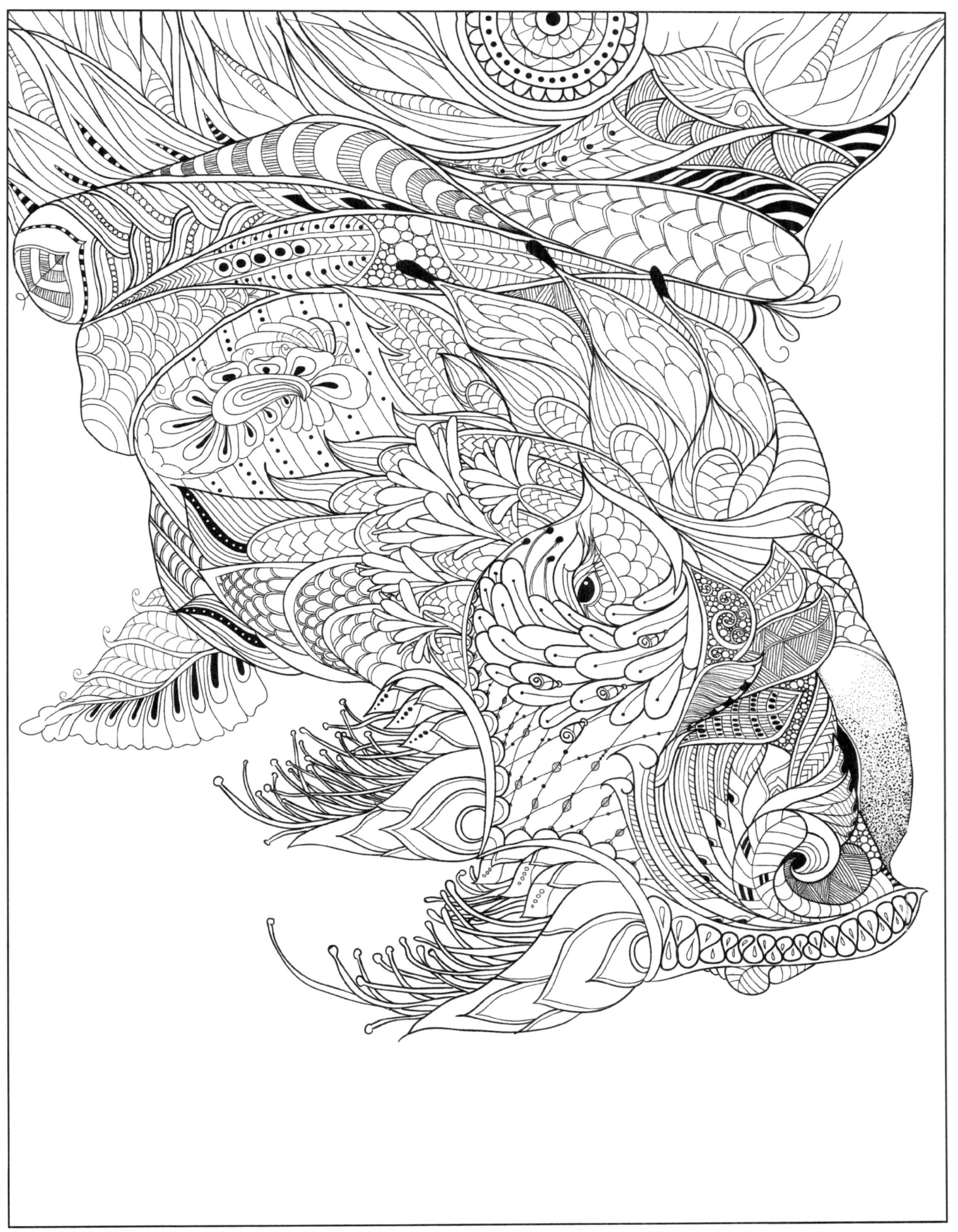

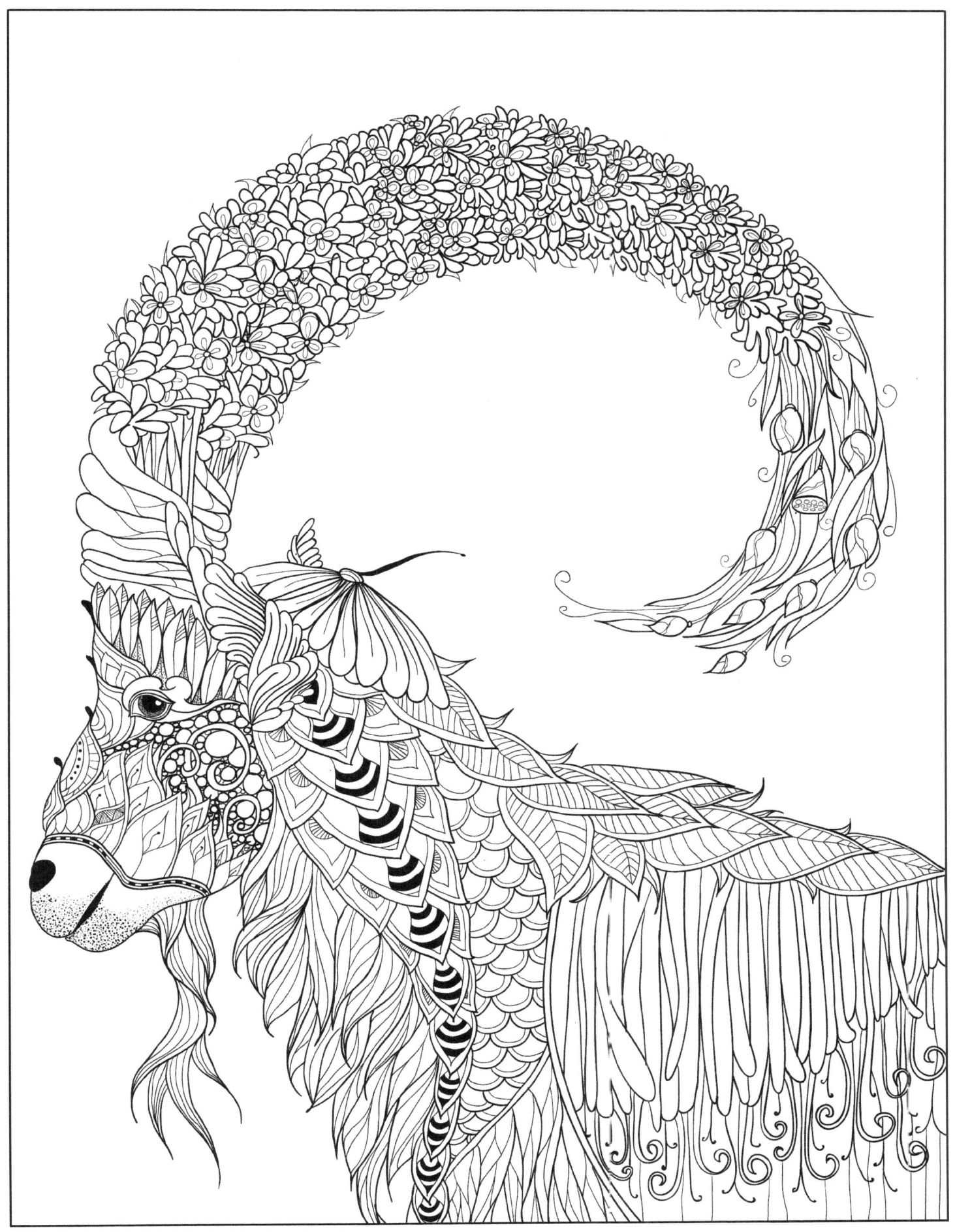

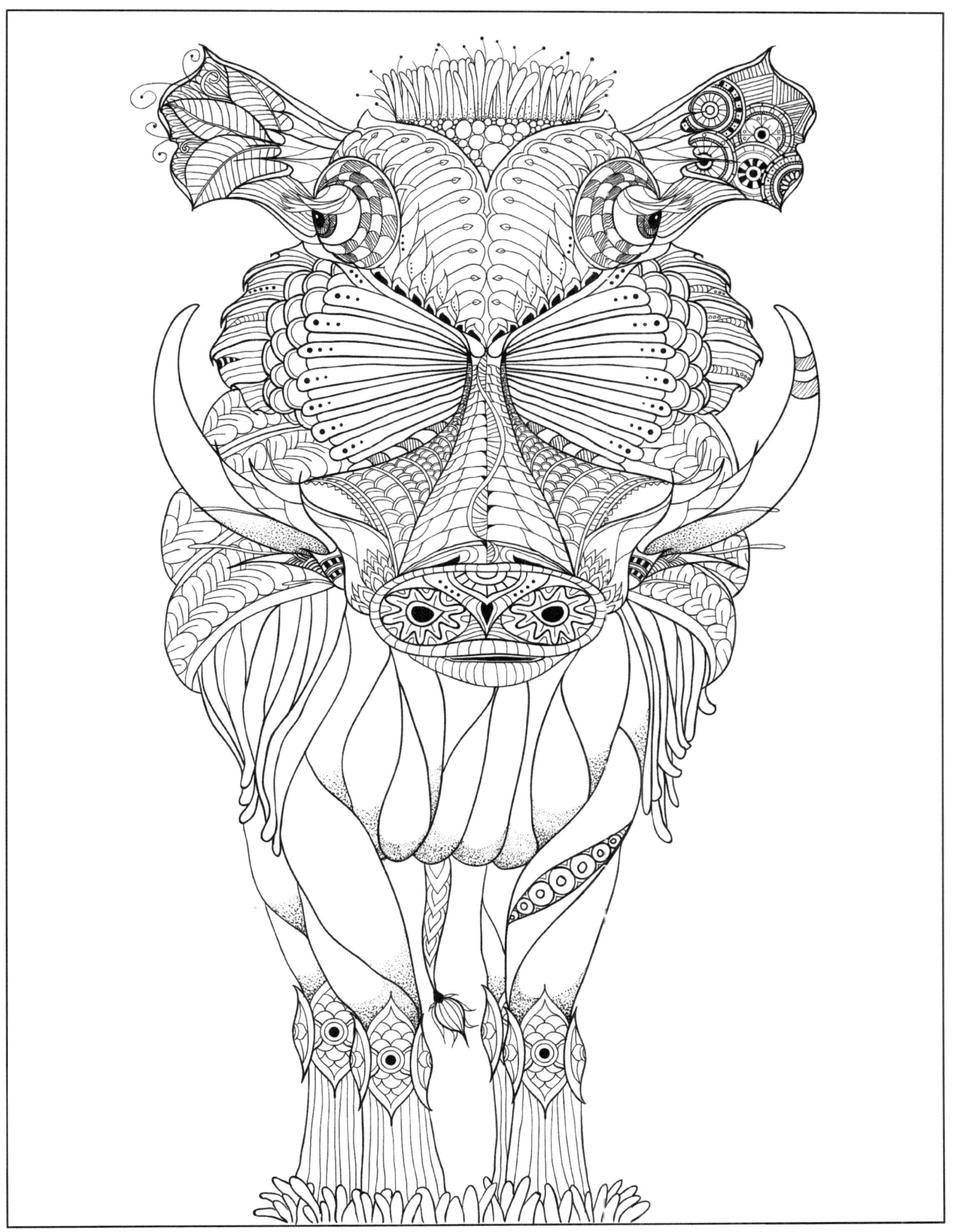

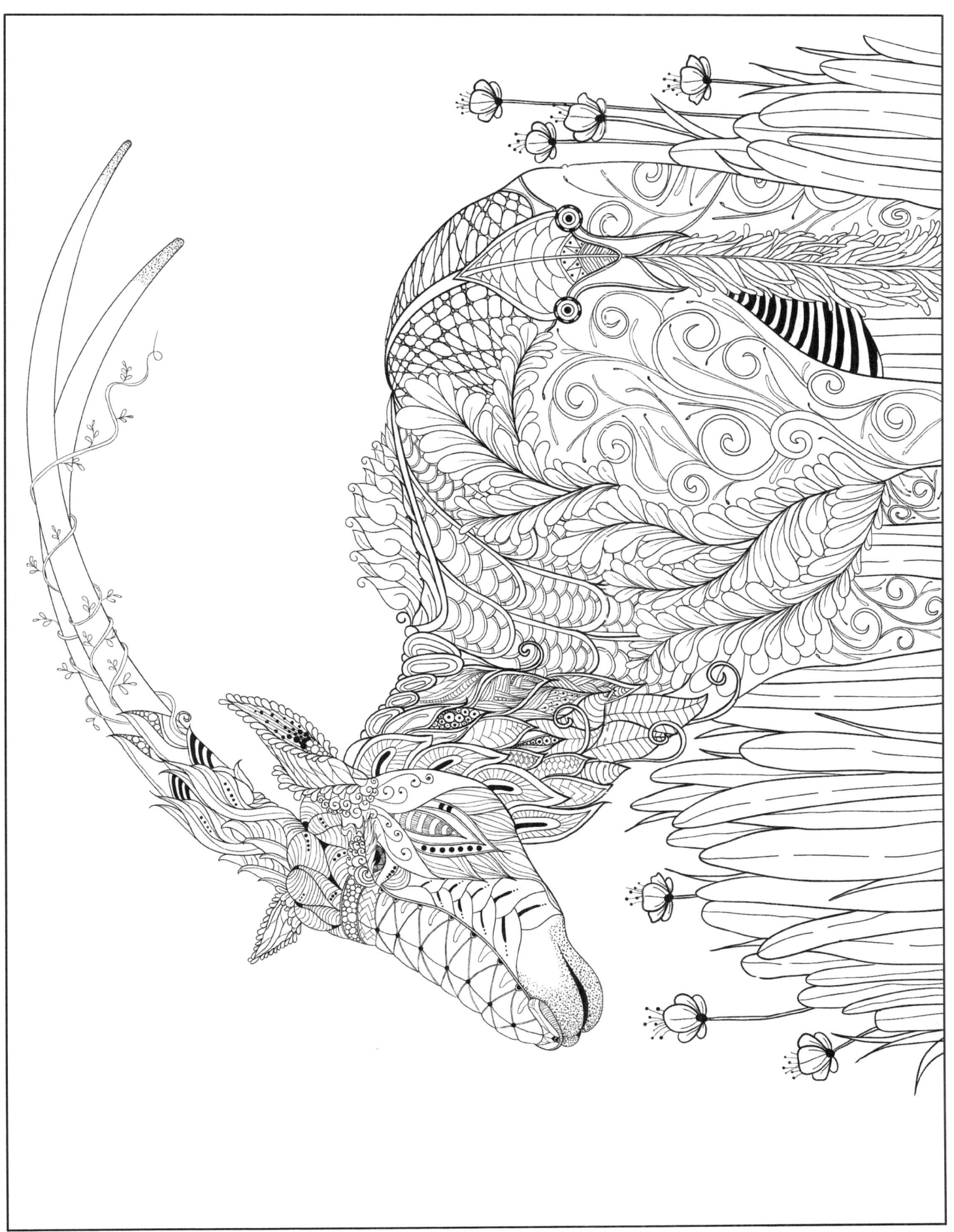

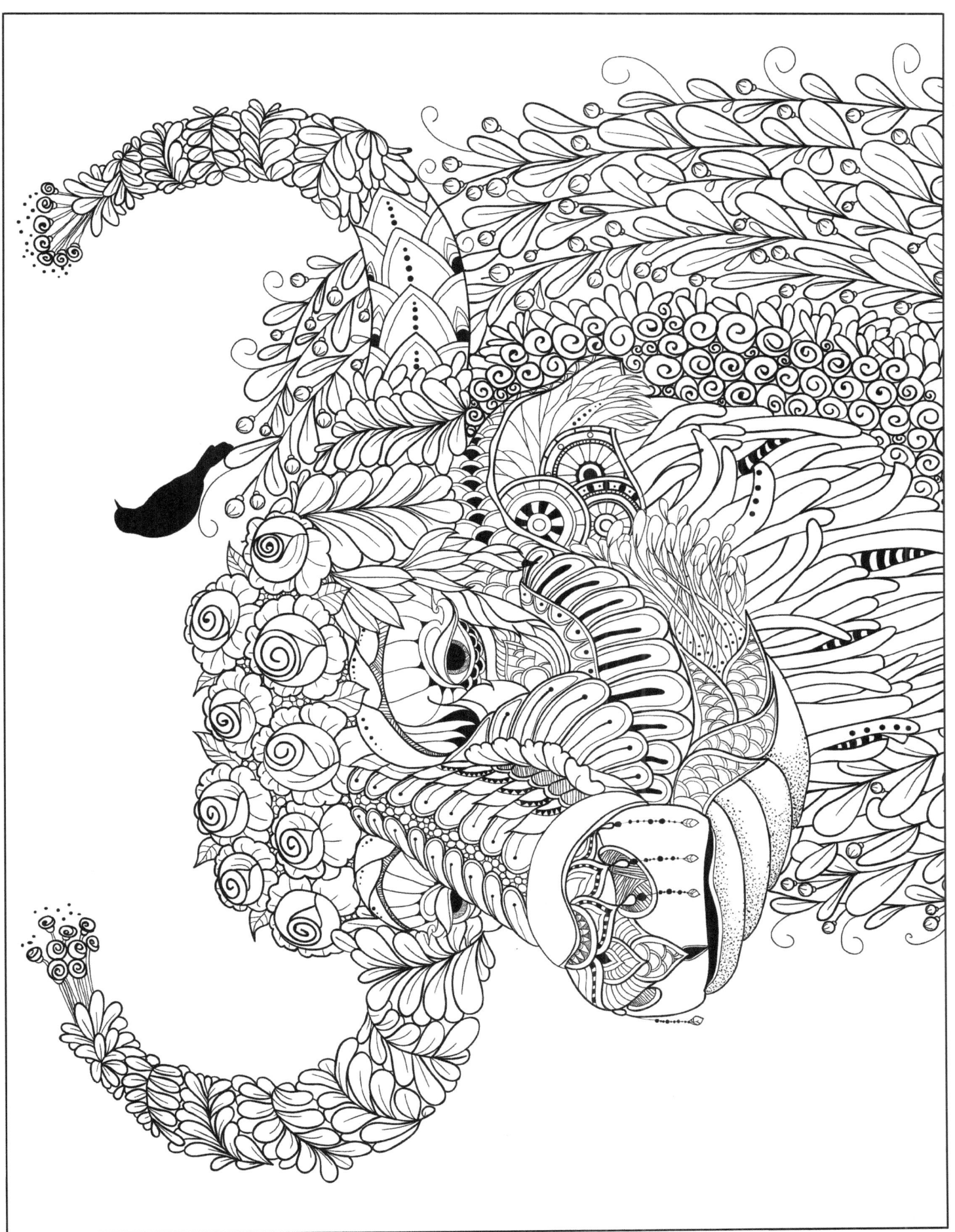

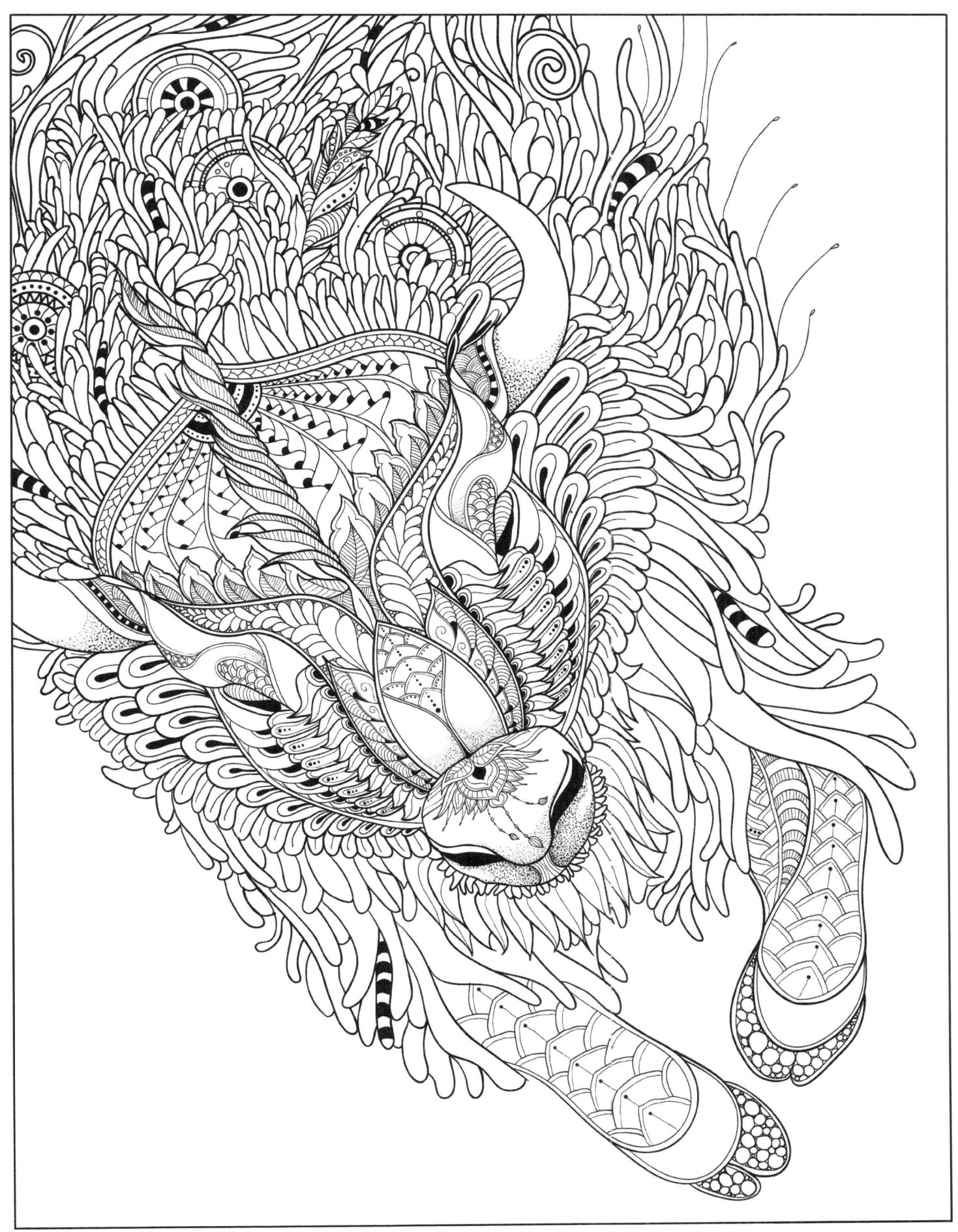

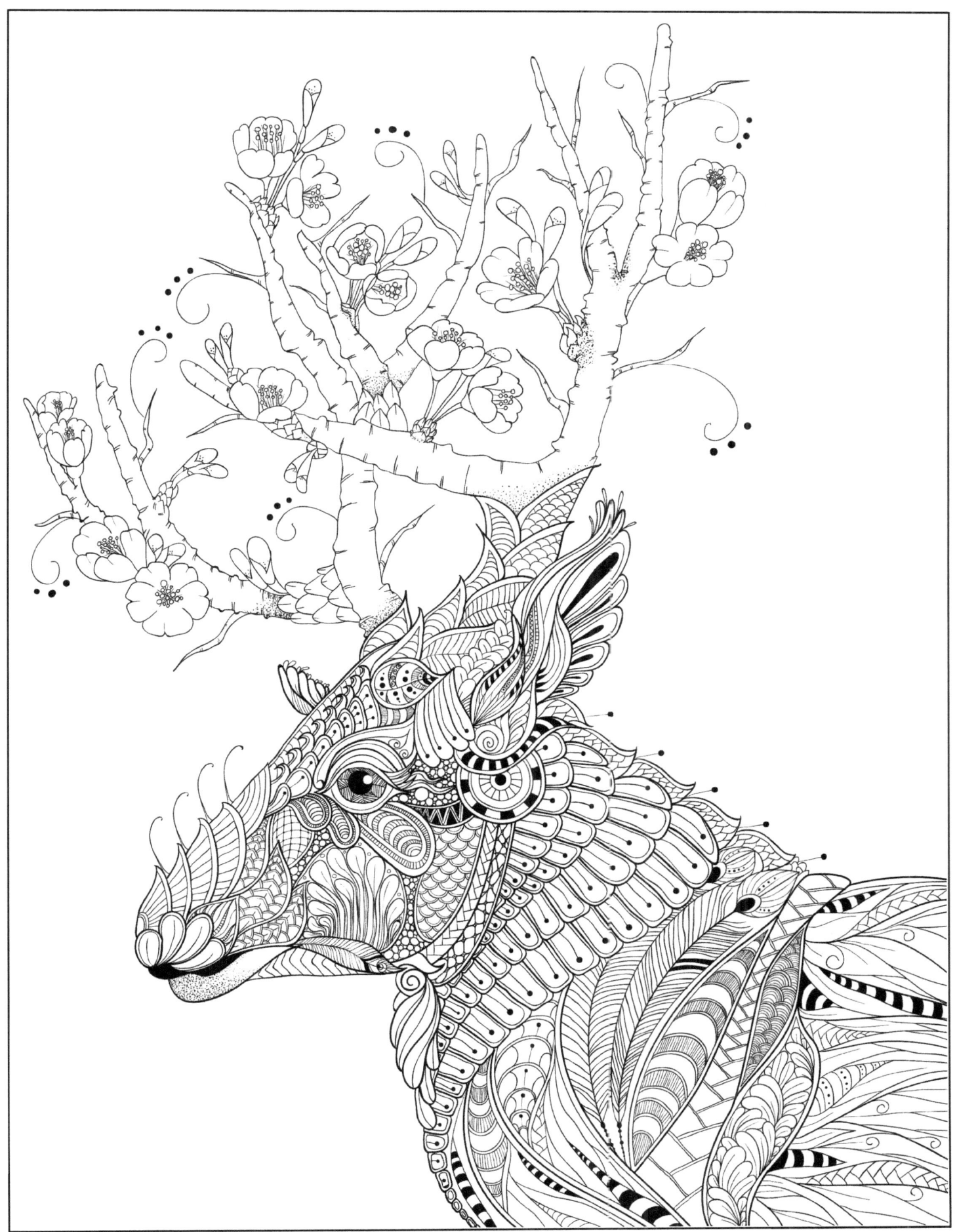

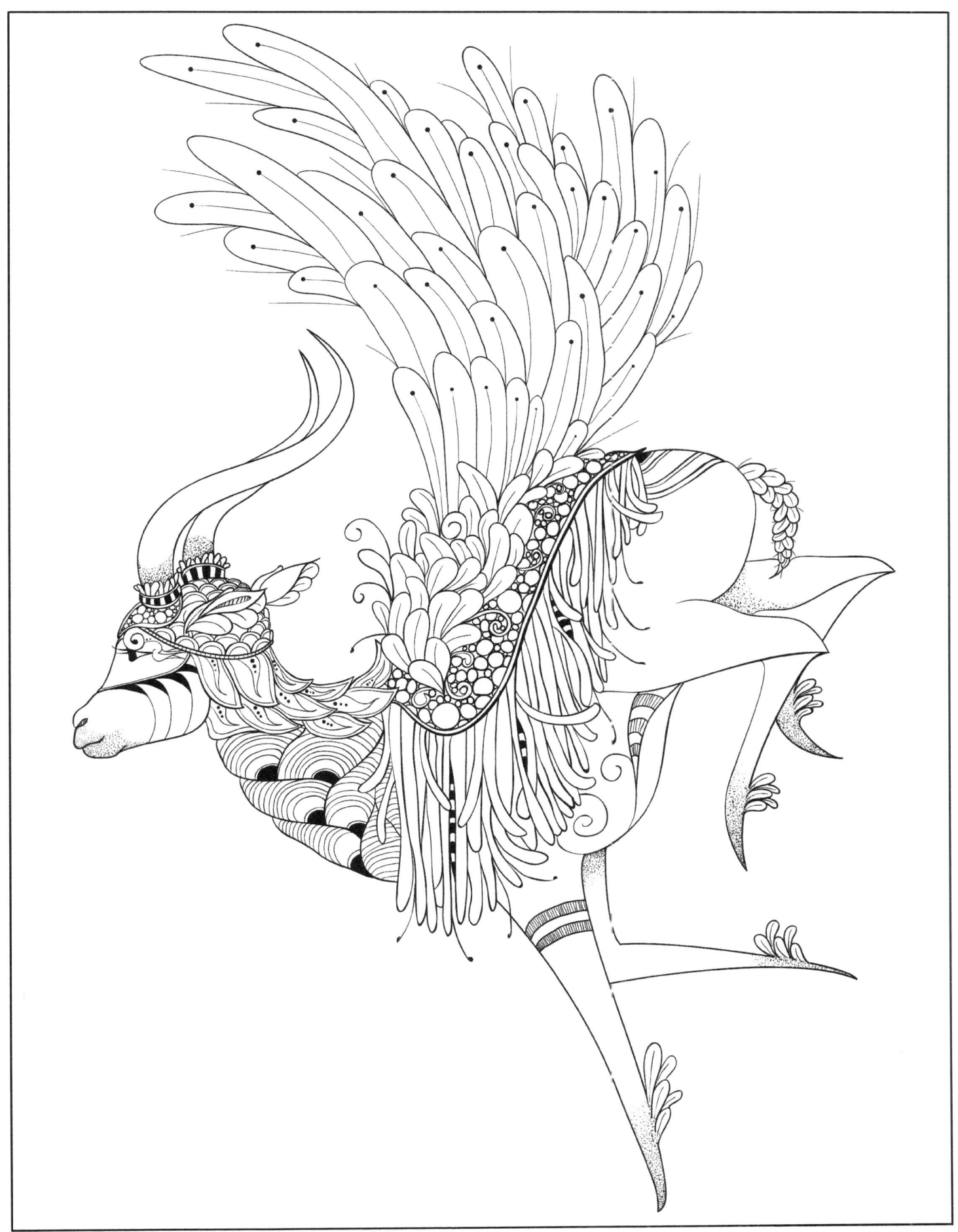

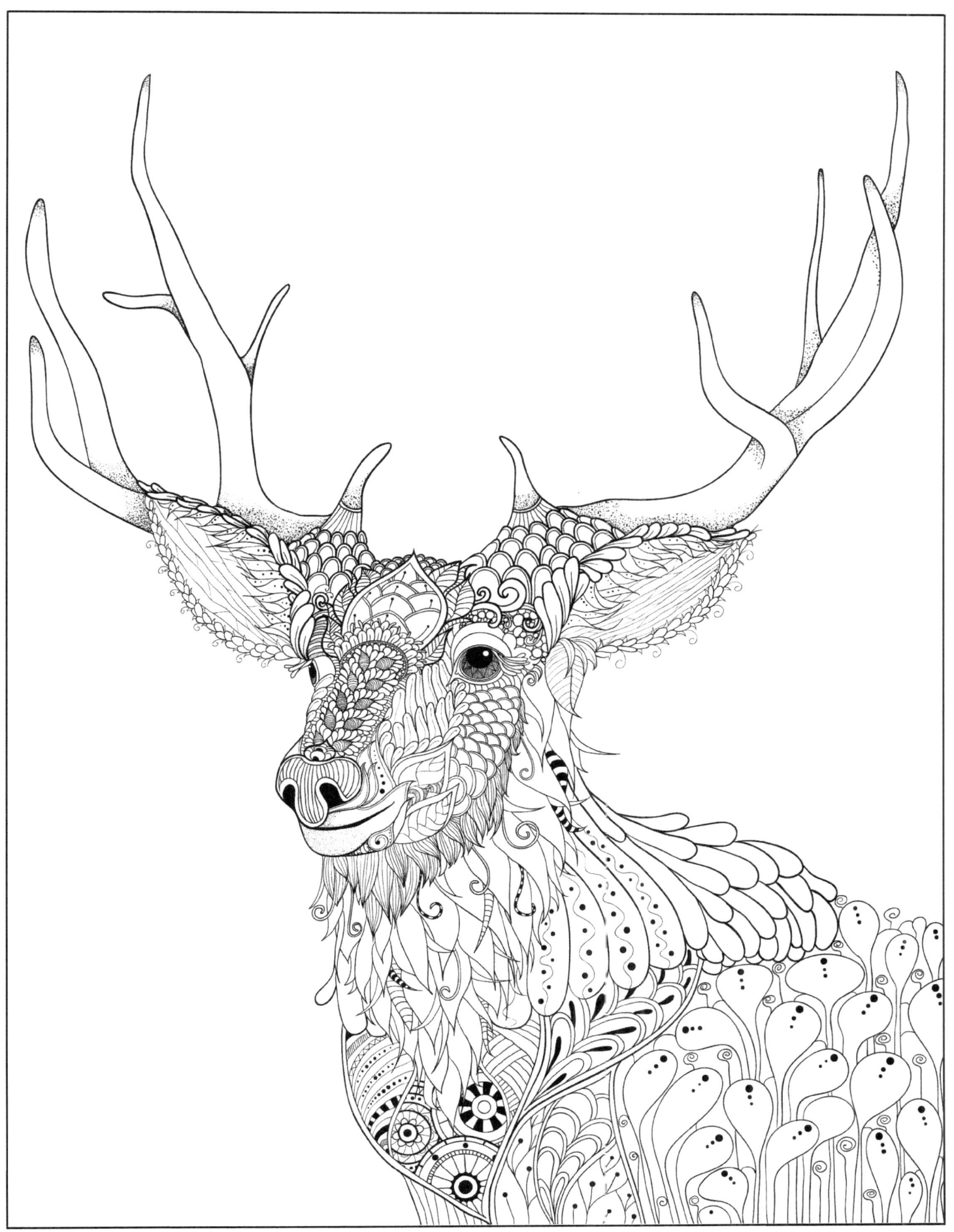

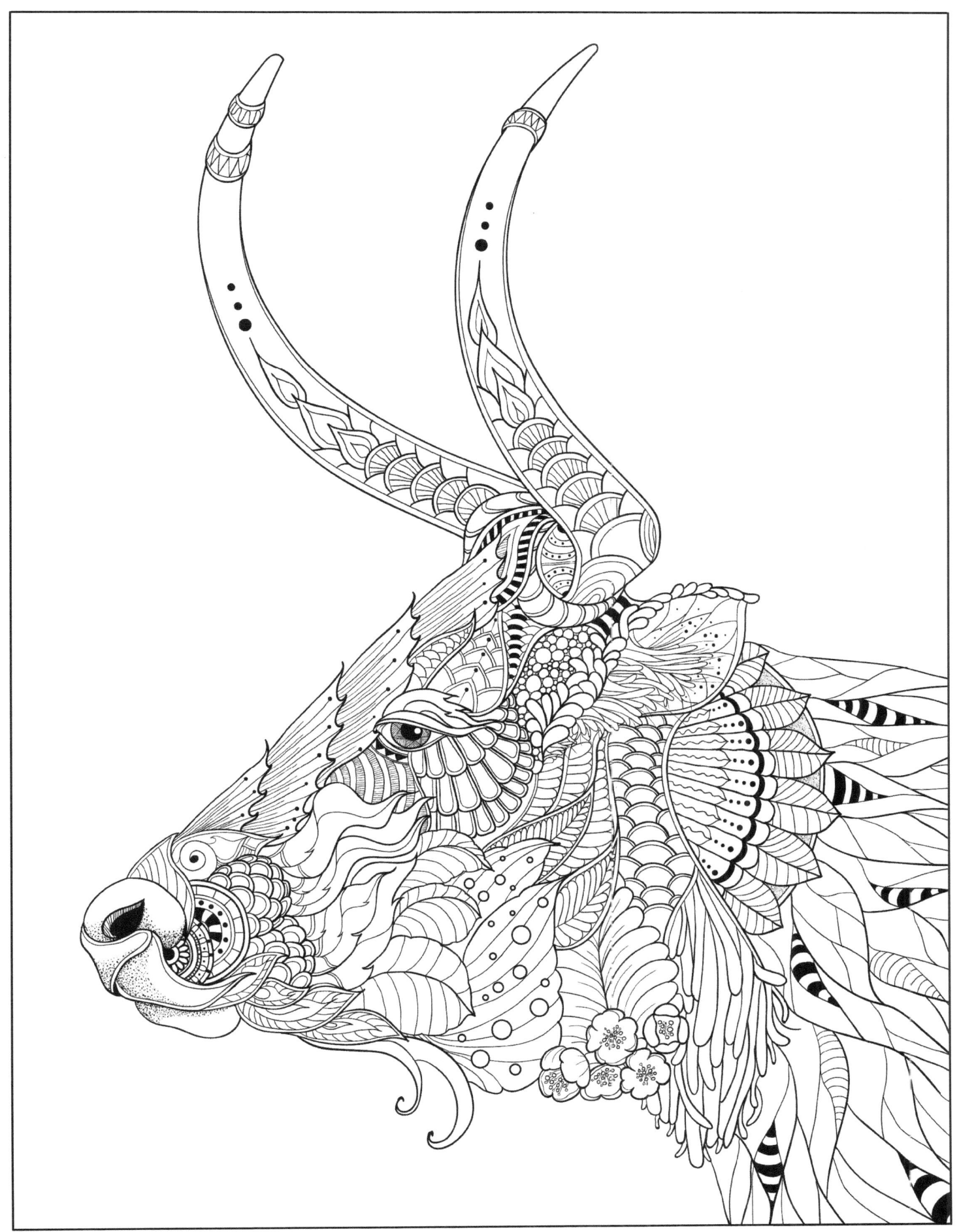

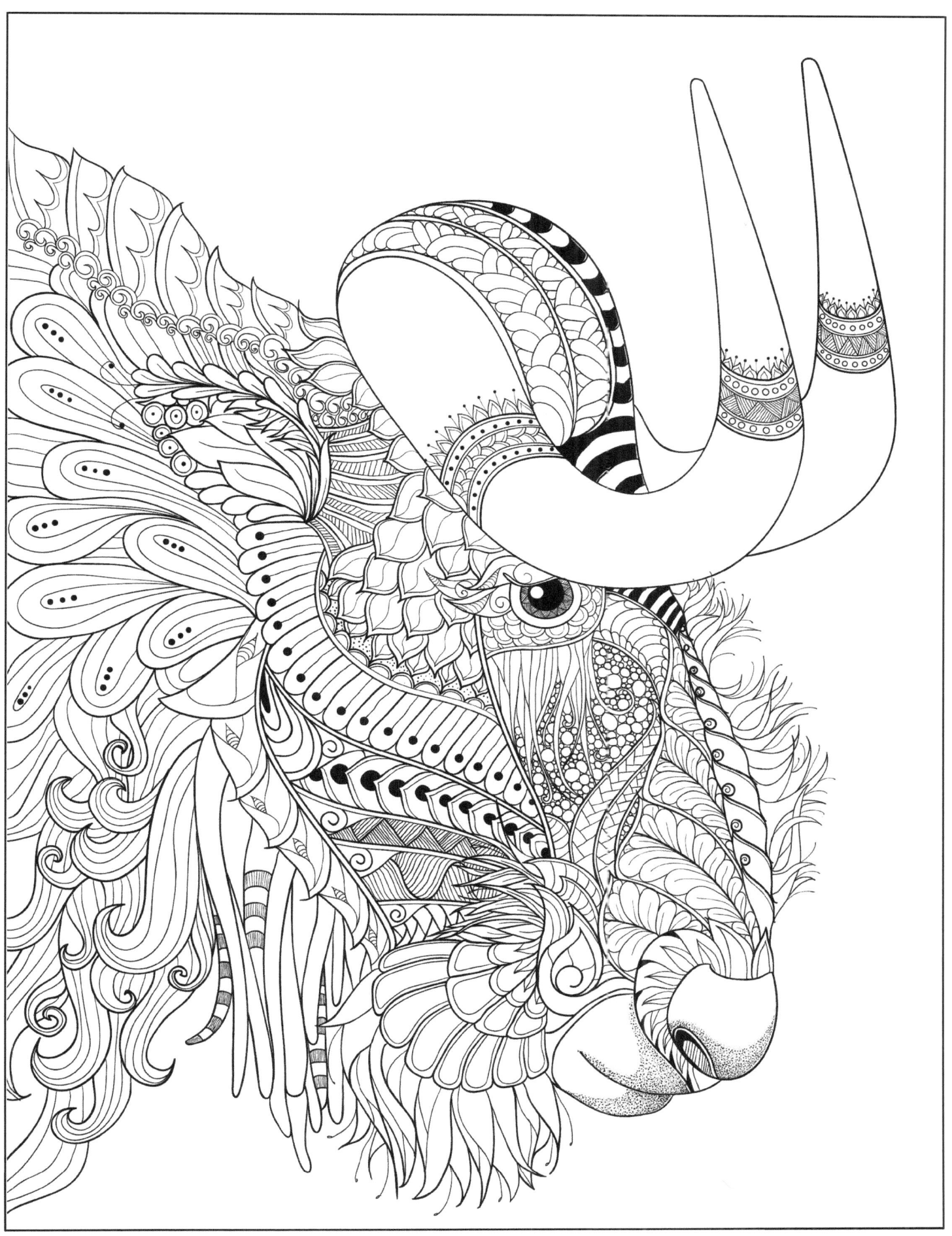

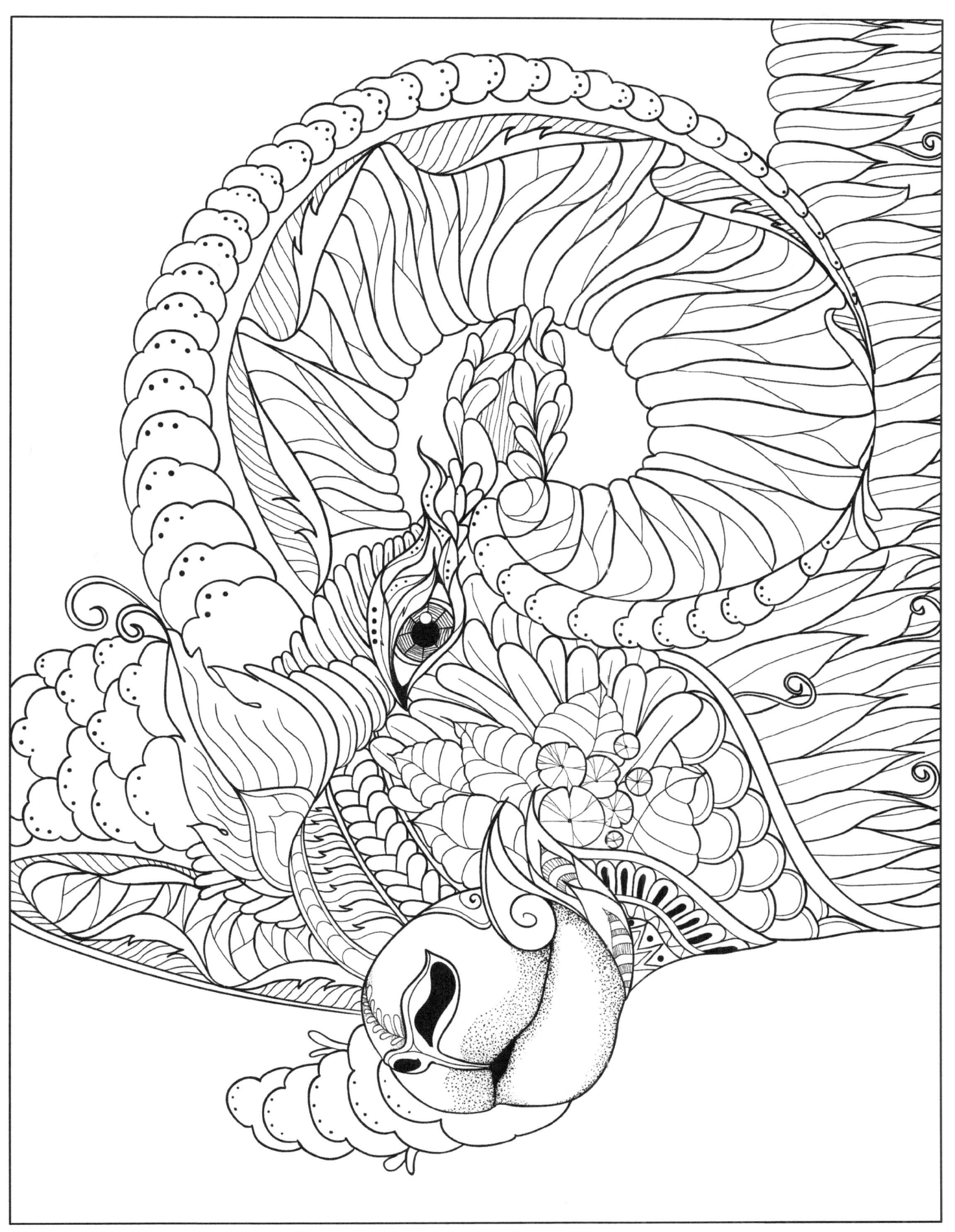

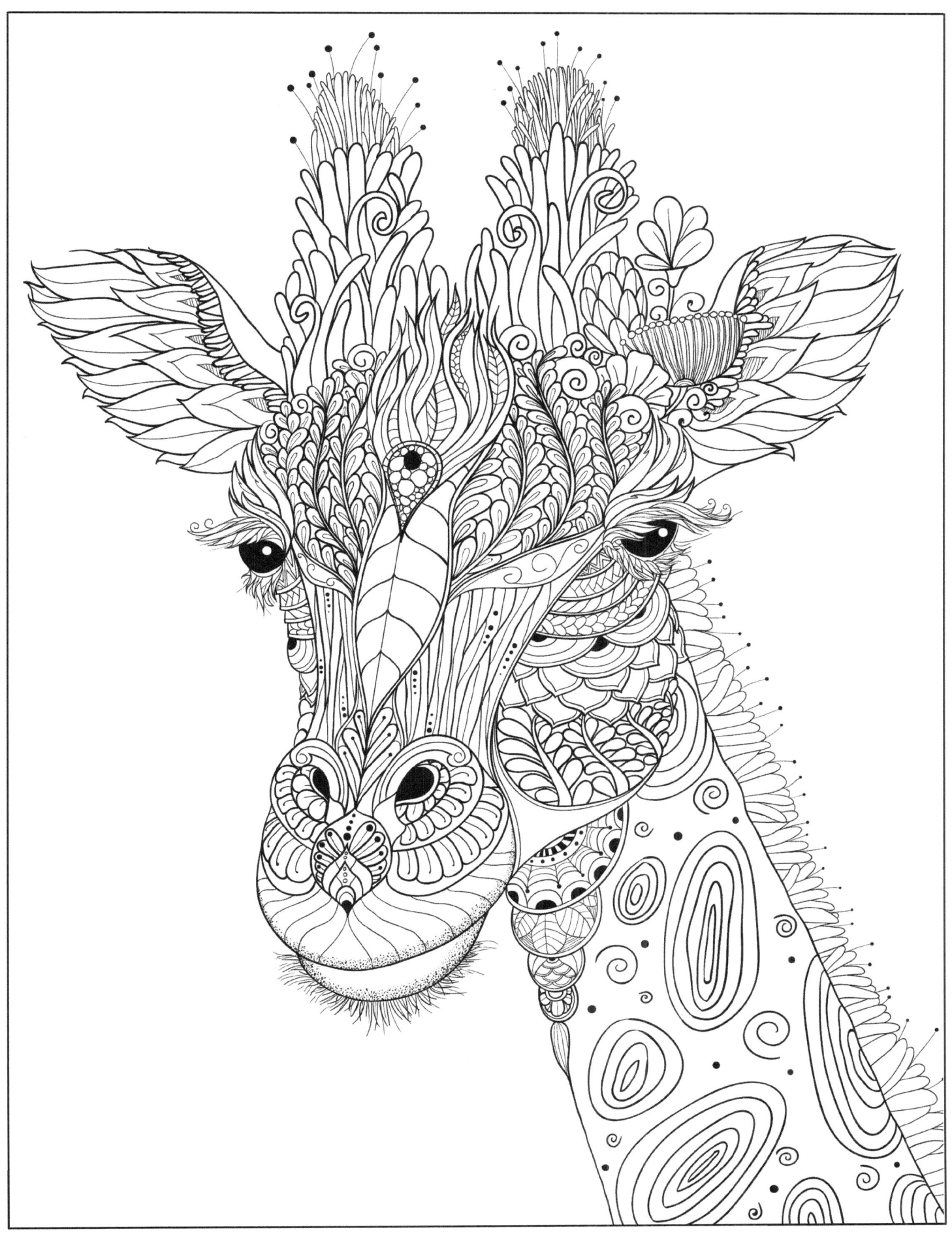

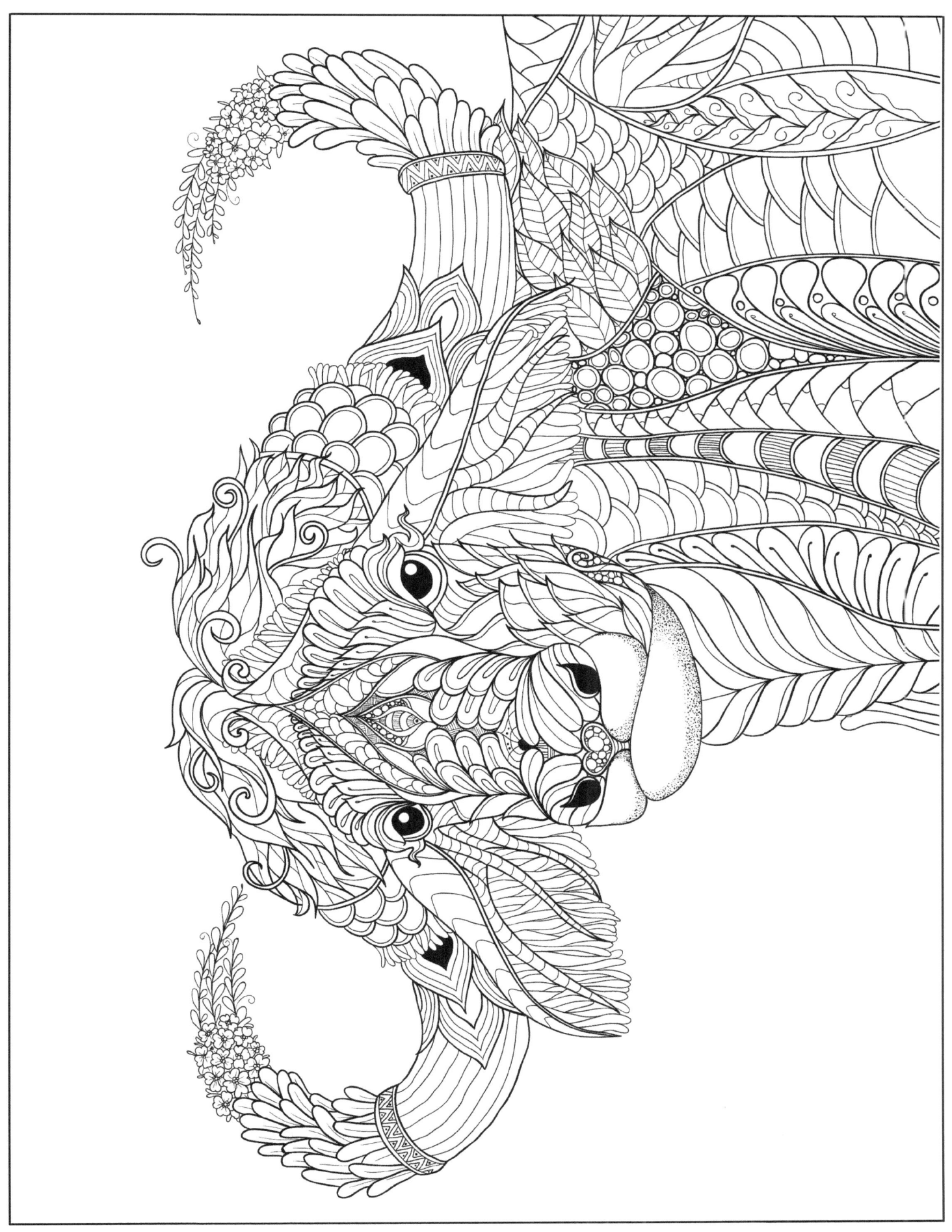

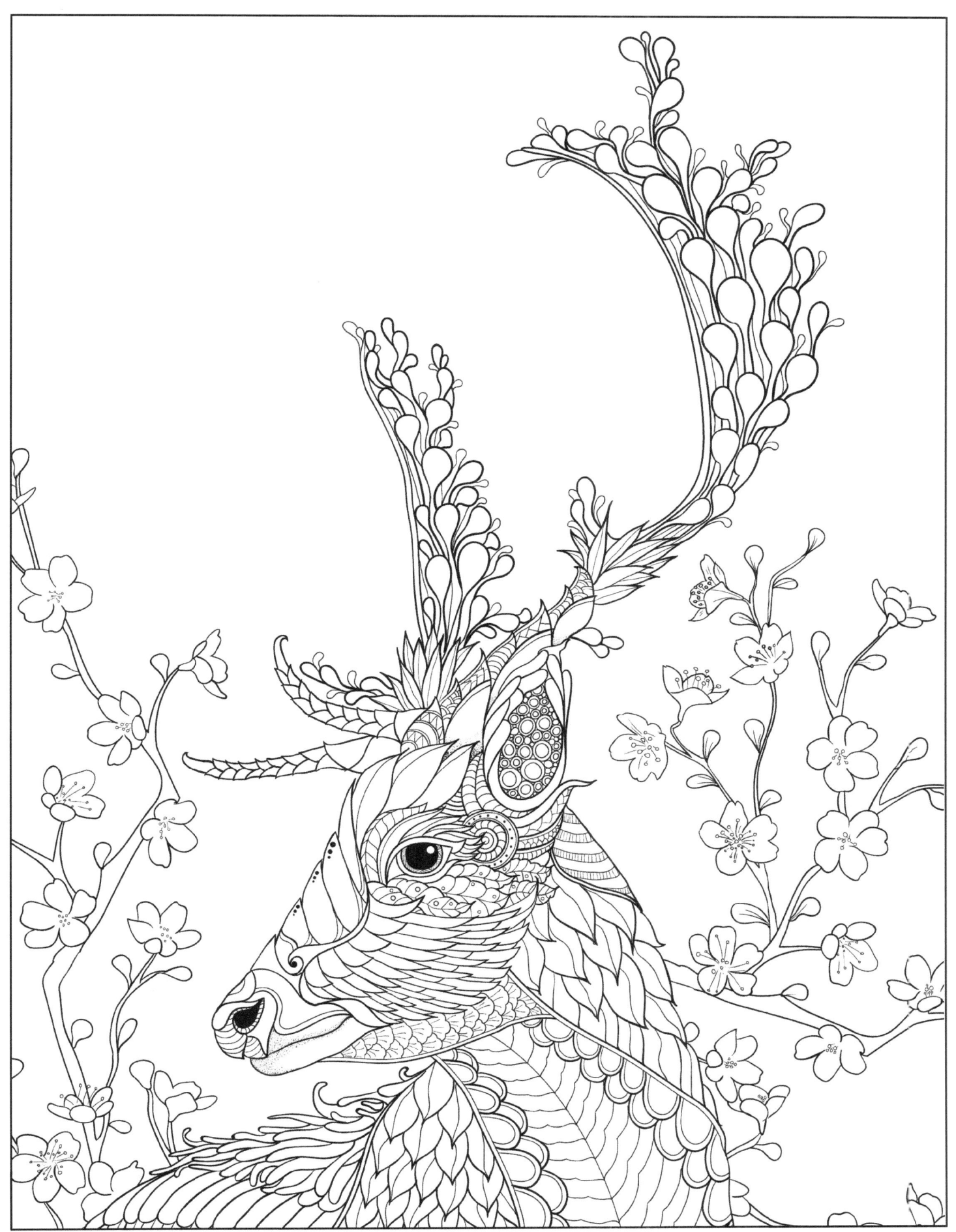

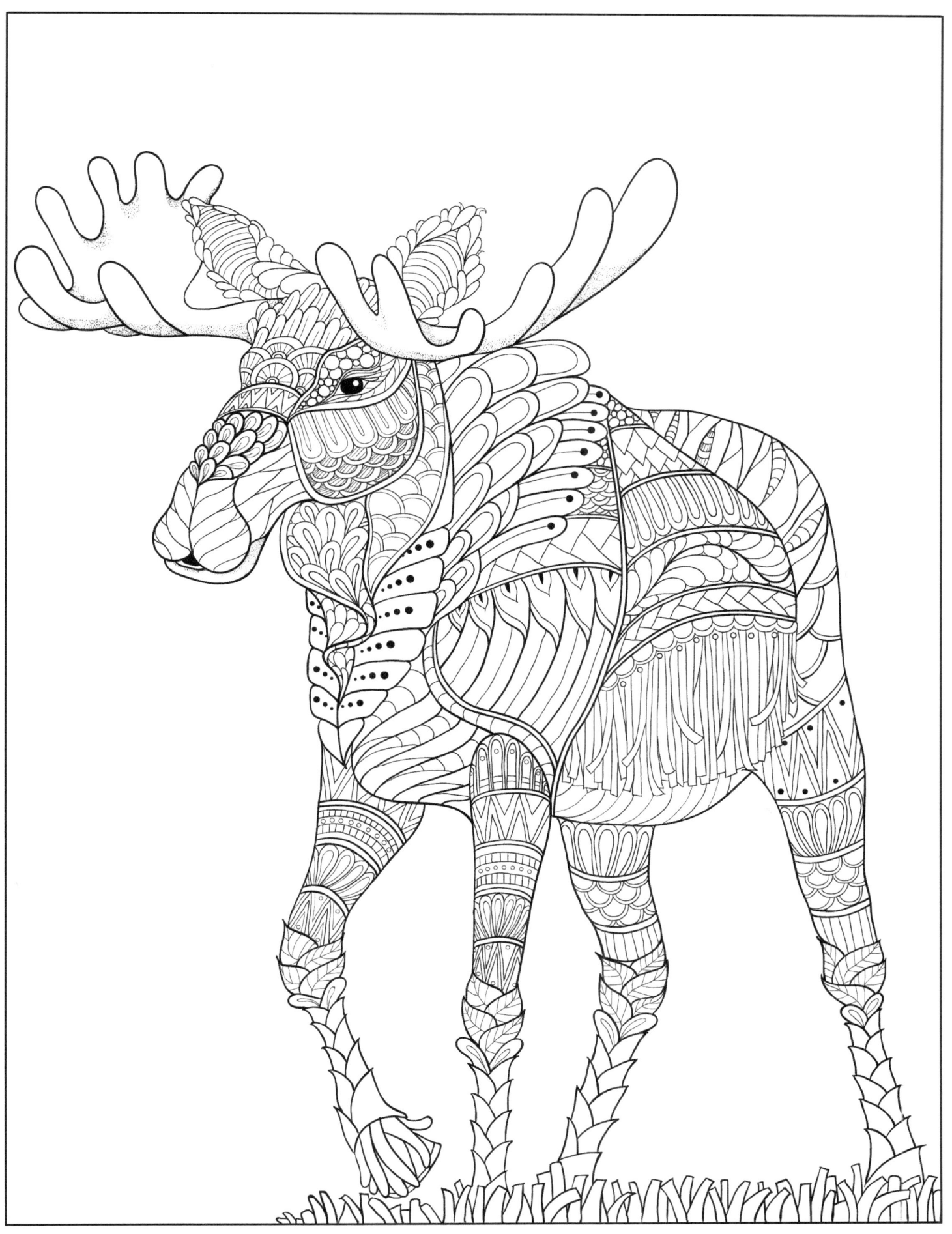

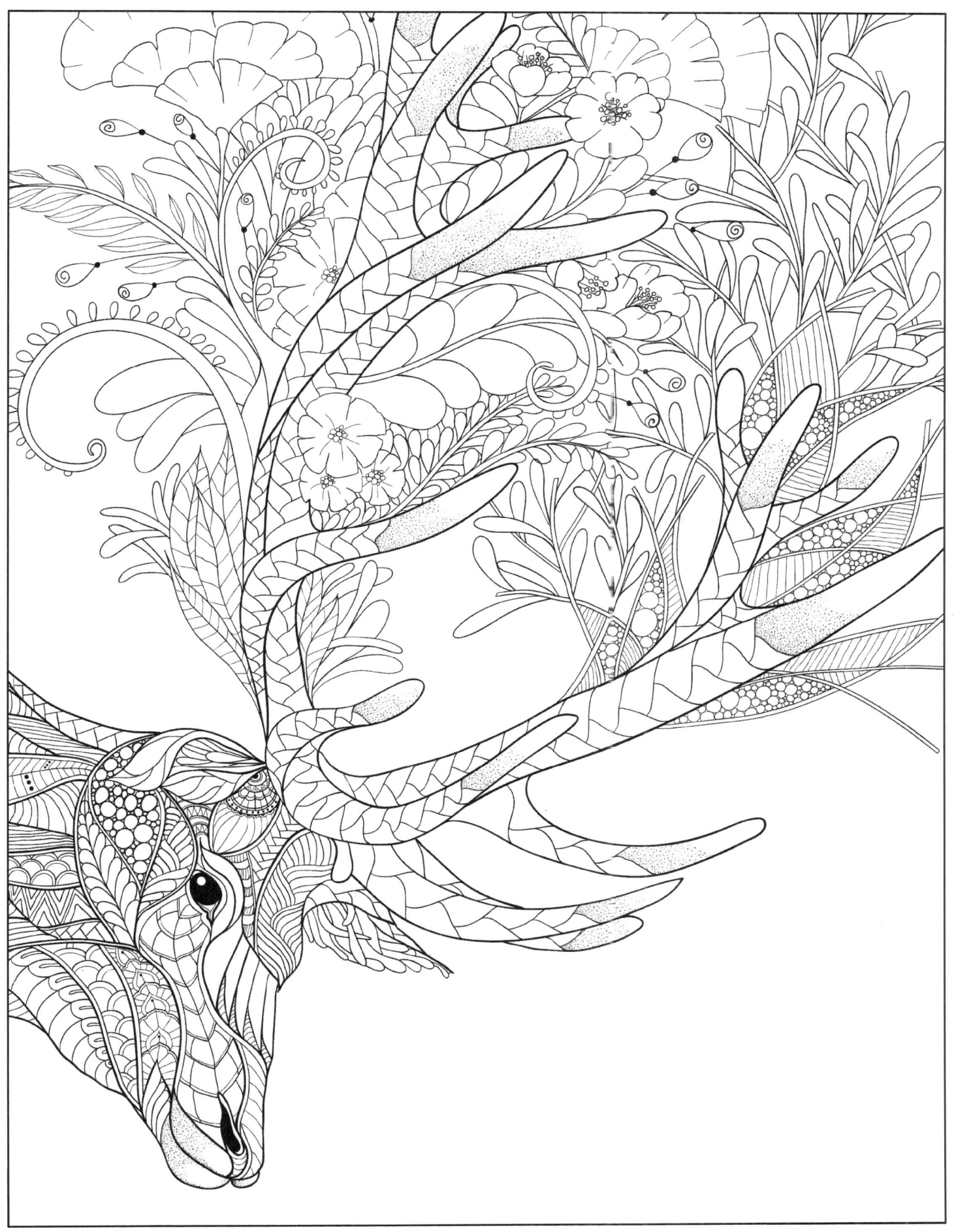

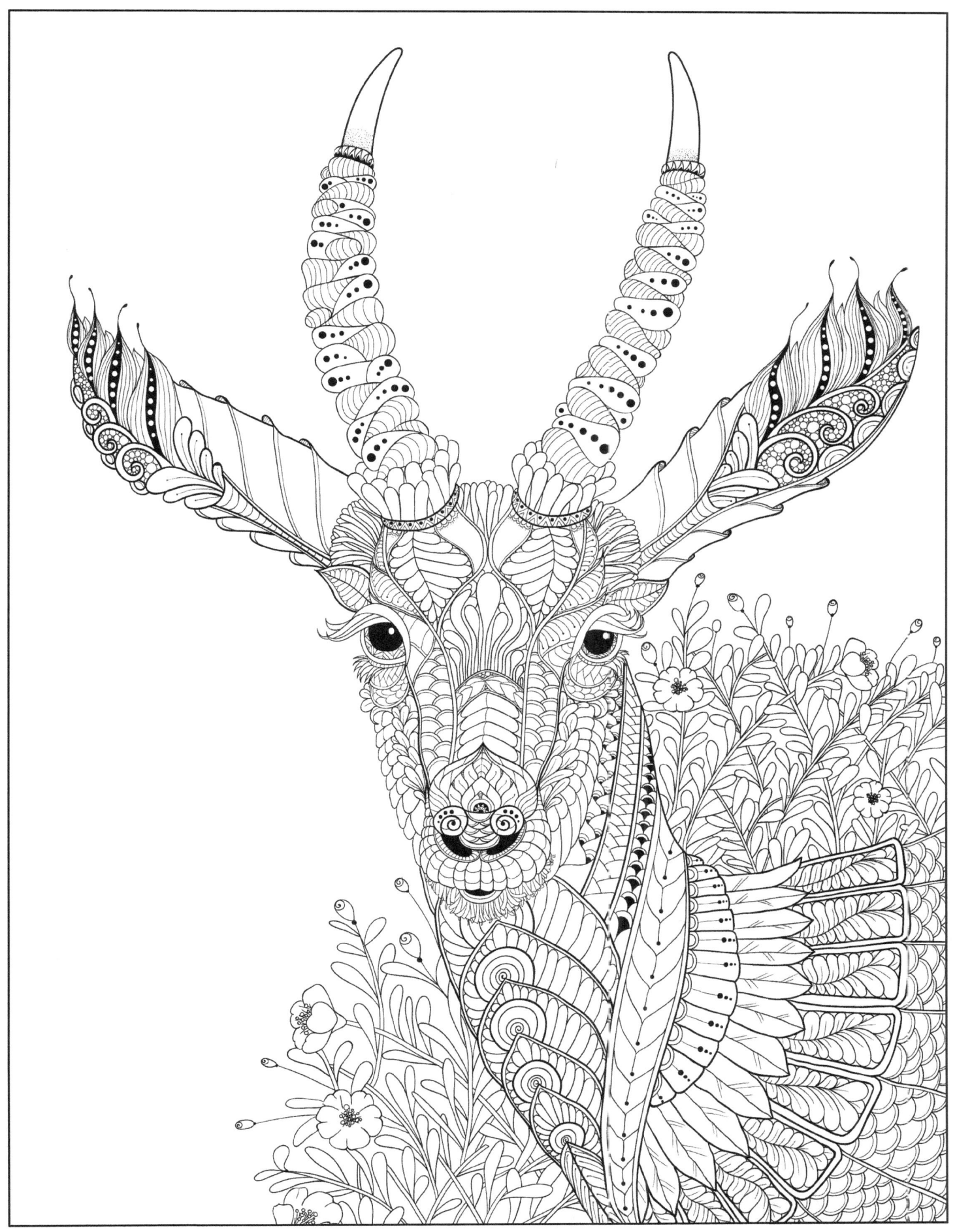

GET FREE OUR COLORING PAGES and Promotion Update

At : bit.ly/get_gift_coloring

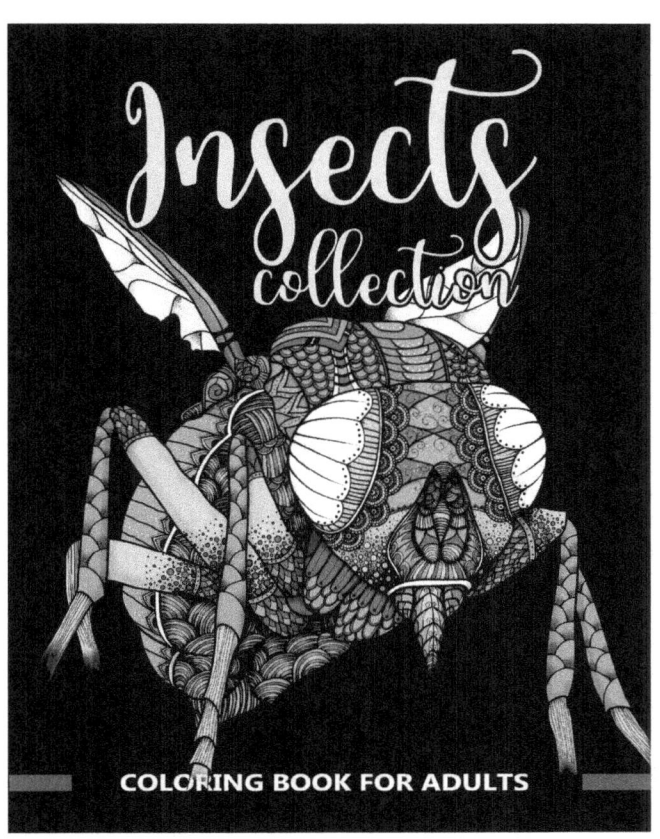
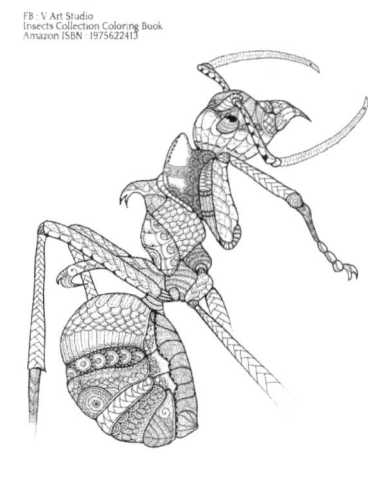
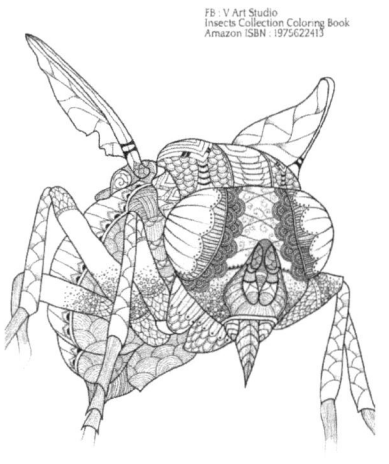

Insects Collection Coloring Book

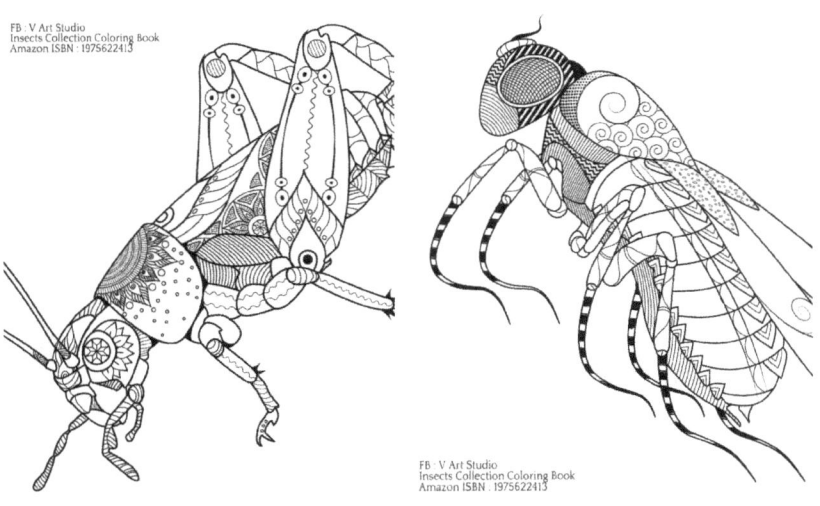
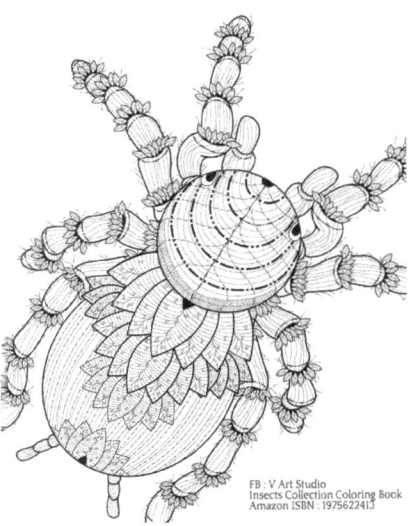

www.ingramcontent.com/pod-product-compliance
Lightning Source LLC
Chambersburg PA
CBHW062124220526

45471CB00010B/3875